THE SLAUGHTER
OF THE KINGS

THE SLAUGHTER
OF THE KINGS

Anya Miller Hall Author of *Discerning Your Season*

iUniverse, Inc.

New York Lincoln Shanghai

The Slaughter of the Kings

iUniverse books may be ordered through booksellers or by contacting:

iUniverse
2021 Pine Lake Road, Suite 100
Lincoln, NE 68512
www.iuniverse.com
1-800-Authors (1-800-288-4677)

Because of the dynamic nature of the Internet, any Web addresses or links contained in this book may have changed since publication and may no longer be valid.

The views expressed in this work are solely those of the author and do not necessarily reflect the views of the publisher, and the publisher hereby disclaims any responsibility for them.

Unless Otherwise Indicated all scripture quotations taken from the authorized King James Version Copyright @ 1961 Finis Jennings Dakes

ISBN: 978-0-595-46128-8 (pbk)
ISBN: 978-0-595-90429-7 (ebk)

Printed in the United States of America

This book is dedicated to every spiritual strategist, warrior and intercessor that has ever come into contact with the dragon lords of this worlds' systems. It is especially dedicated to those called and faithful *Apostles* and *Prophets* that encounter the arcane daily and yet continue undaunted. Most of all it is dedicated to *Lord Saboath*, Mighty Warrior and Conquering King! You, O' Lord, reign supreme!

CONTENTS

Thank You

I'd like to first thank the **Lord Jesus Christ** who procured my salvation and who is everything to me. I also would like to give God thanks for the *"spirit of revelation"* which worketh in me. As always, I thank my children, **Dakisha** and **Trevon**, for sharing me with the world! It is my desire to make you proud of me. I also thank God for my *beautiful grandchildren*, those that are here and those that are yet to come. I am proud to be your Nana! *Thank you for all the hugs snuggles and kisses! Smooches!*

To my brand new son—in—love **Michael Octavius**, *thank you* for loving my daughter and her children and making them your own. *Mummie loves and appreciates you!*

I also would like to thank **P. Stefan Gilliam**, who helped me with the research for this book. Thank you for the *hours* you spent on the phone relaying information. You truly are BIG COUNTRY! This one is for the "Bantu" people! *Mungu Bariki! Busu!*

To the Proton Believers of *Rhema Prophetic Worship Ministries, Inc.*, Thank You for allowing me to be your Pastor! Your growth has been amazing and I heartily encourage you to continue in the *"ruach"* of God. *Don't let the enemy raid your threshing floor!* I love you much! *God loves you even more!* So, whatever you do, *never ever* give up! You are proton believers! First to war, *first* to win, *first* to pray, *first* to praise, *first* to worship, *first* to prosper, *first* to succeed, *first*....

And as always, I must thank my parents, ***Benjamin F. and Myrtle C. Miller.*** They both have gone on to be with the Lord, however, the lessons they taught me are still intrinsically instilled. They adopted me from birth and *immediately* began to shape and mold me for destiny!! From my mother's mezzo soprano and proper speaking voice to my father's humor and warm camaraderie I received a rich legacy of which I am proud!! I *made sure* I told them before they left and I *pray* somehow God will let them know now that they are gone: Thank You for Everything!! *I Love You Much!*

Ms. A *(That's what they called me ...)*

Acknowledgements

To **acknowledge** is to recognize as being *valid*, an expression of *appreciation*. *Appreciate* comes from the word *appraise* which means to determine the value of. I have determined that the following persons have been of great value in my life and have proven to be valid, true, genuine and sincere over the extended period of time that I have known them.

Prophetess Runette C. Jones my friend and an anointed Prophetess whose words never fall to the ground. Thank you so much for everything! Most of all, thank you for your consistent prayer for me and my children. I love you! **Give the Lord a cheer!**

To Apostolic Bishop Leonard T. Smith, (Glendale), *my brother, my rock and my friend.* You are such a soldier! Keep pursuing faithfully the vision that the Lord has set before you even though many will look upon you and underestimate your greatness. I, however, do not. You are one of the most powerful, profound and prolific clarions of God's

Word for this hour that I know! **Keep Walking the Chairs For Jesus!** You know who you are! (**Hint:** *"Luke, I am your father!")* I love you!

To **Apostle Debra T. Giles**, General of Warfare and Intercession! **You are a tenacious warrior at great cost.** You know they say that the best athletes "play hurt" and I suppose that the mightiest warriors *fight wounded,* however, it is my prayer that God will heal the hurt in the *deep places* of your life, so that the great destiny that God has for you will be realized in its fullness. *May God cause all your long awaited dreams to come true!* I love you!

To a **very dear friend** who stays on her *"prayer bones"* for me. You have not only lent yourself, you have also lent your ministry to pray for, give to and encourage me. *Thank you so much for your love* and your **"Big Sister"** talks; they keep me going! **Apostle Rachel L. Harris I salute you!** May all your life expectations be realized to the fullest! "It's **CANDY** time!"

Refuge, Sanctuary, Hiding Place, Safety and Blanket of Love!! All this and more describes the *"progressive family church; with a down home country feel!"* Your love and faithfulness down through the years has ministered to me in a deep place. Thank you for everything, *especially the prayers* and of course the beach! Much love to **Bishop Louis** and **Pastor Mary Brown** and the True Holiness Church of

Ebro, Fl, with *special love* and mention to my Ebro Armor Bearer—**Sherry Brown!**

"Faith, faith, faith just a little bit of faith! You don't need a whole lot! Just use the little you've got!! Faith, faith, faith just a little bit of FAITH!!" I know those are the words of an old Pentecostal church song we used to sing *back in the day*, but they are also words that epitomize who you are and your walk with the Lord!! You are living, breathing, and walking faith!! That's right! I'm talking about YOU! **Prophetess Phyllis Morton**, an Apostle of faith if I've ever met one!! Thank you for standing strong and being a beacon of faith for the Body of Christ!! I know it's been an ever increasing challenge of faith for you these last ten years; but in spite of it all the **EVIDENCE** of your faith speaks for itself!! Here's a shout out to Big Daddy and the Solid Rock Family as well. *I Love You to Life My Sister Sister!* P.S.: *"Come on out of that box and be yourself!"*

To **Apostle Robbie and Pastor Grace Baxter** and the **Perfecting Praise Ministries Family**: thank you so much for *always* embracing me with such welcoming and loving arms. I really appreciate knowing that I have a place of **covenant friendship** where I am *celebrated* and not just tolerated. Much love to you always! *Sniff.... sniff.... Does anybody smell fried chicken???*

Thank you Shepherd Mother Carla Alston for all you've done for me and mine. You are greatly loved and will always be remembered. Never forget, you are anointed to *cover the shepherds with care.*

Apostle Paul and Prophetess "Dame" Ida Thornton you are two of the Lord's staunchest generals. *There is much new territory to conquer!* So, gird up your loins and take possession of your destined domain. Thank you so much for being my friends.

Finally, to **Drs I.V. & Bridgette Hilliard:** my life has been so awesomely impacted since I became an AIM Pastor. You are greatly loved and appreciated. Thank you for all that you do.

Foreword

"The Slaughter of the Kings" is a *must read* for those who have an Apostolic anointing upon their lives. This book gives insight and revelation into the principalities of fear, war and the occult which are invading the earth, the church and our individual lives. As the Kingdom of God moves forward, we need to understand our enemy, his purposes, and his plans. As you read this book, it will expose the plot and mindset of Satan towards the church. It gives a detailed scriptural and historical perspective of these principalities, how they came into ruler-ship, and what we must do as an apostolic army to slaughter them.

Slaughter of the Kings reveals a *fresh strategy* on how to overcome the spirit of divination, the spirit of religion, and the spirit of perversion that has invaded our government, church and society. Those who are called to the Apostolic are challenged to come forth in their anointing and destiny in order take back what the enemy has stolen from believers. We are in the midst of an Apostolic Restoration where God is strategically raising up Apostles all over the earth. He is repositioning Apostles globally in order to address these demonic forces that are trying to infiltrate and take over God's people. If the Kingdom of God is going to advance in the earth, Apostles must come forth in their power and authority. If you are not a warrior, then this book is not for you! Slaughter of the Kings provokes you to war! As I read this book, I was provoked to another level of warfare. *My apostolic mindset was challenged to advance the Kingdom at all costs while retrieving from the enemy what he has stolen from the church!!*

I've known Apostle Hall and her ministry for several years. She *indeed* is a true example of an apostolic warrior. She not only wrote this book out of a revelation perspective but also a personal perspective. She understands what it means to war and to win! As you read this book, get ready for your next level of victory!

Apostle Paul Thornton
Paul Thornton Ministries International
www.ptministries.org
apostle@ptministries.org

Introduction

This book is based on Genesis the fourteenth chapter, the account of Abram returning from the slaughter of the kings. Rich with prophetic symbolism, this passage of scripture reveals the confederacy of prevailing ruling spirits in the world today. And, so, as in the days of Abram, who is an apostolic type, this confederacy must be destroyed.

The times that are upon us are more crucial than ever. Ancient evil is on the rise as demon monarchs *re-strategize* and release hoards of *trans-mutated principalities* with incredible power. Seducing spirits entice the masses with the opiate of the supernatural and thrust them drunkenly into the realm of the unknown.

Slowly, insidiously, a dark kingdom emerges from the shadows ruled by forces whose reach encompasses the four corners of the earth. This encroaching blanket of iniquity has invaded every level of society from the poorest to the richest, from the ignorant and uninformed to the intellectual giants of the day. Something must be done!

Despite Herculean efforts of those on the front line of warfare, minions of the enemy have been defeated only to be replaced by ravenous hordes of miscreants with greater power to deceive. Thus, our pre-emptive strike must be more powerful and precise. The time has come for the apostolic fathering anointing to arise with greater intensity; *once again,* it is time for the slaughter of the kings.

THE PROVOCATION

What would it take to move you from relative comfort into aggressive pursuit of the enemy? For Abram it was the attack upon and ultimate captivity of a loved one. Sadly, that is what it usually takes for the average Christian to arise from a mundane and mediocre lifestyle of tepid faith.

Lot, Abrams' nephew had been captured by armies of the *four king confederacy* led by Chedolaomer, King of Elam. They had ruled the Siddim Valley and surrounding areas for twelve years. At the end of twelve years the Kings of Sodom, Gomorah, Admah, Zeboim and Zoar rebelled. Thus, Chedolaomer and his confederacy unified their strength, revitalized their strategy and began a campaign of conquest. Razing the land, they attacked and defeated some of the most terrible adversaries of their time!

The rule of these *four kings* for *twelve years* represents the apostate and counterfeit apostolic move in the earth. For, while they defeated giants, possessed territory, over-threw kings and built nations, they did so through demonic powers and perverse motives. Their end was not to glorify the God of creation but rather to glorify themselves while establishing satanic power as the governing authority.

Sound familiar? These same tones are being sounded within the fabric of today's society as moral attitudes are shaped and soldered into place by the blacksmiths of depravity. These arcane forces violently raid our countries, governments, communities, schools, churches and most of all our homes. In the second chapter of Statistics of Democide by R. J. Rummel it is stated that "pre-twentieth century killing—massacres, infanticide, executions, genocides, sacrifices, burnings, death by mistreatment and the like for which corpses had been counted and estimated add up to a range of 89,000,000 to slightly over 260,000,000 million men, women and children dead." The 2000 UN Commission on the Status of Women reported that globally, at least one in three women and girls have been sexually abused and beaten in their lifetime.

Many times the kingdom of God turns its head while chaos is perpetrated all around. From the killing fields of Rwanda, Sudan, Cambodia, Auschwitz and Iraq to our very own cities, towns and communities; the people of God are insulated by blankets of apathy that keep them from being involved. That is, until, like Abram the enemy attacks them or their family. It is then that the apathetic blanket is cast off and the spirit of the warrior arises.

This is the provocation that goads the people of God *out of religious comfort* into radical apostolic pursuit and dominion. These luciferic kings must be destroyed and only the armies of the Lord can do it! So arise, pursue, overtake and recover all!

KINGSHIP

In any war it is imperative that one knows what they are up against. Underestimating the enemy is a *deadly* mistake. Warfare is more than brute force and requires acute stratagems and tactics, effective weaponry, skilled warriors and sagacious leaders. Thus, defeating the enemy requires that we gain knowledge of him. The Apostle Paul states in II Corinthians 2:11 "that we may not be over-reached by the Adversary, for of his devices we are not ignorant." (Young's Literal Translation) Therefore, if our battle is against a confederacy of kings we must first ask and answer the question: what is a king?

The definition of king is as follows: a male monarch, one who is the most powerful and prominent in a group or place. This last definition is most significant in that one must be able to identify the "king" in their life, home, community, ministry, state and nation. Who or *what* is the strongest and wields the most power?

A monarch is the sole and absolute ruler of a state, a sovereign, one that presides over or rules, one that surpasses others in power or pre-eminence. The Hebrew word for king is *melek* and means royal and to reign. The Greek word for king is *basileus* and means a foundation of power; established. Thus, *kingship is a foundation of established power that rules pre-eminently over a place and its people.* It is this foundation of power that *supports* the throne and the king on whose head the crown rests is simply *a puppet* of that power. Therefore, in our quest to slaughter the kings we must uncover and demolish the power or principality *behind them.* "For we wrestle not against flesh and blood, but against principalities, against powers, against the rulers of the darkness of this world, against spiritual wickedness in high places" (Ephesians 6:12).

Whoever and whatever is king in your life and region is ruled and supported by a foundation of power; a principality. If the dominant "king" is *wicked* and *demonic* in nature the foundation of power is satanic.

When kings are crowned into positions of power they fund their domain by gathering riches through *taxation, war* and *plunder.* This means that willingly or unwillingly the people of the land are used to *finance* the malevolent reign of a demonic king.

Finance is the science of the management of money and other assets, banking, investment and credit, monetary resources and funds, especially those of a government or corporate body, to supply the funds or capital for and to supply funds to. The etymological and *literal definition* of the word finance (*finis*) means *to end, a payment in settlement of a fine or tax* and to *pay ransom*. Thus, the financial policy of a king can tax, make difficult excessive demands upon the populace and hold them hostage.

The USAID Financial Marketing Development Report states that "the primary role of the financial system in *any* economy is to mobilize resources for productive investment." It further states that "an efficient financial system channels resources to activities that will provide the highest rate of return for the use of the funds. These resources stimulate economic growth; they provide enterprises with the ability to produce more goods and services and to generate jobs."

Adversely, wicked kings enact financial policies which do the opposite. A good example of this is the Congo; potentially one of the wealthiest nations in Africa because of enormous reserves of gold, copper, cobalt, rubber and more. In 1965 Joseph Mobutu seized power and began to take all that he could up to an estimated four billion dollars. He was overthrown by the Rwandan army in 1997 leaving his country among the poorest in the world and declared insolvent by the World Bank. (Pillage and Plunder: An Anthology of African Dictators, Marc Roberts)

Similarly demonic kings seize power over a region and its people and begin to build finance for their regime by placing excessive demands upon them through living expenses, medical bills, lusts, addictions and indulgencies. These are things that people need or think they have got to have. It is the desire for these things and more that hold the populace hostage and motivate them to pay the ransom demanded.

Ransom is paid when someone or something of value has been abducted and held on threat of injury or death. The person from whom the ransom is demanded is manipulated and virtually held prisoner by the abductor. Hence, the degree and quality of livelihood is affected by the reigning king's financial policy.

Therefore, *finance is the throne* upon which the king sits and the foundation of power, (principality), *behind* the throne controls and manipulates the economic climate of the land in order to gender capital that empowers the king's reign.

Thrones of Power

Chedorlaomer, King of Elam

The head of the four king confederacy was Chedorlaomer, King of Elam. Chedorlaomer means *the servant of Lagamar* or *handful of sheaves.* Lagamar was an Elamite goddess of the underworld who received the souls of the dead. Therefore, Chedorlaomer prophetically represents the *spirit of a demonic reaper.* A reaper is one who goes in with a sharp cutting instrument and gathers that which has been produced. This spirit cuts down everything you try to accomplish. You sow; labor and wait patiently only to have everything fall apart before your very eyes.

Reapers go in only when the harvest is ripe. Ripe is defined as that which is mature and sufficiently prepared. It also means *opportune.* The reaper spirit waits until everything is in place for you and all things seem to be on the verge of working out. You are filled with excitement and anticipation when *suddenly* out of nowhere, the reaper attacks, severs all plans and eradicates opportunity. The spirit of the reaper is also known as consumption.

For, not only does it devour harvest, it influences the person to begin to consume it as well through gluttony, greed and unwise spending. This spirit alone has discouraged and disheartened multitudes to the point of despair. The will to try, to plant and produce has been broken. Personal dreams and goals have been abandoned and replaced by a less than mediocre automaton existence. The reaper spirit is cruel, merciless and strikes without warning. It leaves behind a *spirit of failure* upon the land and upon the people.

"And so it was, when Israel had sown, that the Midianites came up, and the Amalekites, and the children of the east, even they came up against them; And they encamped against them, and destroyed the increase of the earth, till thou come unto Gaza, and left no sustenance for Israel, neither sheep, nor ox, nor ass." "And Israel was greatly impoverished because of the Midianites; and the children of Israel cried unto the Lord." Judges 6:3-4, 6

The above account is an example of the reaper spirit. The Midianites and others would wait until Israel had sown and the harvest was ripe to swoop in and destroy it. Verse four states that these reapers "left no sustenance for Israel." The Hebrew word sustenance in this scripture is *michyah* and means preservation of life. The reaper spirit devours and destroys that which is necessary for the continuation of life. It not only affects ones existence but erodes the quality of life as well for Judges 6:2 states that Israel had taken to living in caves and dens because of the Midianites.

The reaper Chedorlaomer was the king of Elam. Elam comes from the root word *alam* that means to hide and to secrete. The word occult *also* means to hide, cover and keep secret. Thus, the foundation of power or principality behind the reaper is the occult. The occult is a principality that promotes concealment; accomplished by spirits of darkness, obscurity and surreptitiousness.

Consider the Ndrangheta; Wikipedia, The Free Encyclopedia states that it is "one of the most powerful and ruthless crime organizations in Italy." A federation of blood families, the Ndrangheta adheres to a strict code of secrecy and silence. It is this cloak of silence that allows them to operate as they do both locally and internationally while reaping gargantuan profits. The Ndrangheta is only one example of how occult and reaper spirits work together. If you look closely you will find them in families where molestation, abuse and incest occur, in schools, businesses and even the church. Consider John 3:19 which states that "men loved darkness rather than light, because their deeds were evil." Hence, wherever you find darkness there will be a manifestation of evil. Therefore, anything that is shrouded in secrecy and darkness is occult in nature.

Elam was peopled by the descendants of the second son of Shem for whom the city was named. They are said to be the founders of ancient Persia that today is modern day Iran. They were a nation of people who dwelt in the mountains of Persia, and often rushed *suddenly* down upon the low—lying lands in plundering raids. These vicious reapers were empowered by demon spirits; for, the Elamites were an idol-atrous people.

The capital city of Elam was *Shushan* or Susa. Shushan means "lily" and refers to the lotus, a species of lily that represents the great mother goddess in ancient eastern religions. This is not surprising since the kings of Elam were chosen through a matrilineal system of succession and were referred to as the *"son of a sister."* The king and noblemen had to marry a close relative and produce offspring to inherit the crown. Therefore, incest was a tradition in ancient Iran that was allowed and perversely sanctified. Even though incest promotes retardation, deformation, insanity and other psychological disorders, the Kings of Elam were produced in this manner.

It is suggested that worship of the mother goddess originated in Susa. This stems from the practice of ancient Elamite women, who were cave dwellers, having several husbands during their fertility period. The "husbands" were most often their brothers or sons. Therefore, tracing genealogy through males was almost impossible. One had to be able to show connection with the mother in order to live in the cave. Thus, veneration of the mother was essential for survival.

The mightiest and most renowned of the goddesses was Venus. Venus was known by several names, some of which are Al-uzza, Manat, Al-lat, (which means *"the goddess"* as opposed to Al-lah which means *"the god"*), and the most popular of Elamite culture, Anahita.

Venus was the goddess of music, love, jealousy and coquetry. She was the goddess of love, sexual desire and was known as the "queen of pleasure." She had many lovers and sexual rituals were performed in her honor. It is from the name of the goddess Venus that that the words venereal and *venereal disease* have come. Some of her other titles were the Queen of Heaven, the Mother Goddess, Mother Earth, Gaia and Wicca.

Worship of the goddess included profane sexual practices, sorcery, idolatry and much more. These idolatrous practices tell us a lot about the demonic powers that were active at that time. Spirits of incest, sexual perversion and witchcraft, all of these and more operated under the cloak of the occult to establish a foundation of power for the throne of Chedorlaomer.

Thrones of Power

Tidal, King of Nations

The name Tidal means fear. This kings' name brings to mind the natural phenomenon called a "tidal wave." Tides are the regular fall and rise of sea level in oceans and other large bodies of water. A *tidal wave* is the crest of a tide as it moves around the earth, thus, tidal waves are a *global* occurrence. The word wave has many definitions; however, the one that applies prophetically to this subject is as follows: *a movement that sweeps large numbers along with it.* Consequently, this king brought with him a myriad of phobias, *waves of fear.*

Fear is defined as an emotion of alarm and agitation caused by the expectation or realization of danger. Alarm means to feel apprehension of approaching or existing danger. Agitation is defined as extreme emotional disturbance. Thus, fear was the means by which Tidal exercised his dominion. This indicates that the *spirit of intimidation* is in operation. Intimidation *keeps* its victim in a state of agitation and apprehension. The victim fears that the intimidator will hurt or harm them in some way. Intimidation is a form of witchcraft. Witchcraft is undue influence exerted upon an individual, group of people or place through intimidation, manipulation, and ultimately domination. This is accomplished through emotional, financial, physical, and spiritual means. Therefore, Tidal ruled by the *spirit of fear* empowered by the principality of witchcraft.

Tidal was the king of nations. Nations in the Hebrew is *goy* and means foreign, gentile and heathen. It includes "massing." So, tidal was king of a large group of people who were from various foreign heathen nations. Among them were Samaritans, Phoenicians, and Egyptians.

The area of Tidals' domain was called *Aram*, which means "high", and is today called Syria. Archeologists have found the remains of at least fourteen temples to fourteen different gods dating from the time of ancient Syria. This reflects the polytheistic culture of Arams' mixed society. The main focus of worship was that of the goddess Astarte; also know as Ishtar, Venus and Astoretha. In Aram, Astarte was the mother goddess, and *queen of the prostitutes*. To prostitute is *to solicit and accept payment for sexual intercourse and to sell ones' abilities, talents or name for an unworthy cause.*

While most are acquainted with the sexual aspect of prostitution many overlook the second definition of selling ones abilities or talents for an unworthy cause. For instance, take the marketing, human resources, accounting and sales skills of a drug dealer. These are abilities needed in every business whether it is small or Fortune 500. However, the drug dealer is using his or her abilities unworthily because, for whatever reason it may be, they fear they can make it no other way. Fear promotes prostitution.

Goddess worship culminated at the vernal equinox when day and night are of equal length. The celebration centered around sunrise during which sexual orgies were performed and the Astarte myth also includes the idea of a resurrected sun god; Adoni, her lover, who was worshipped in a sacred grove at daybreak. This same idol later became known as Mithras, son of the mother goddess, who was worshipped on the first day of the week called the "sun day."

Hence, the pagan holiday of Easter and sunrise service originated from the worship of Astarte, as did the tradition of gathering on the 1st day of the week, the sun day, to worship. *(Please note that importance lies not in when you worship but who you worship).*

It is also interesting to note that Jezebel, wife of King Ahab mentioned in the book of I Kings was a Phoenician princess. The Phoenicians were the result of the intermingling of Syrian and Canaanite peoples. Thus, she was born and reared in a matrilineal goddess society where women were revered and ruled through witchcraft and sexual favors. This explains her controlling and ungodly behavior.

The foundation of power behind the throne of Tidal, King of Nations is witchcraft manifested through fear. This allowed King Tidal to *prostitute* the lives, resources and abilities of his people. The land was shackled by the spirit of prostitution.

THRONES OF POWER
Arioch, King of Ellasar

Another partner of Chedorlaomer's confederacy was Arioch, King of Ellasar. Ariochs' name means *the mighty lion* or lion like man. He was called *Bel-Arioch, the god of war.* War is defined as a state of open, armed and often prolonged conflict, involving *strategy* and *tactics*, the deploying and directing of troops. A warlord is a military commander exercising civil power in a given region and a *warmonger* is one who *advocates* and *stirs-up* war. Warmongers amass weapons and wealth thru conquest. Thus, the foundation of power or principality of Ariochs' throne was *the spirit of conflict* manifested through war and the wealth and support of his reign was obtained through warmongering.

It is possible that Mars, the Roman god of war and Aries, the Greek god of war originated from Bel-Arioch. Bel-Arioch was King of Ellasar. Ellasar, formerly called *Warsa* is modern day Iraq. Located in lower Babylon on the site of ancient Sumer, this city is one of the oldest civilizations of the world.

The people of Ellasar or Warsa built their cities around the temple of their gods. They worshipped Shamash the sun god, to whom the city was dedicated. Shamash, called Shamesh in some texts, is referred to as *a male*, and in others, as *a female*. Purported to be the *god of justice*, Shamash supposedly brings wrong and injustice into the light. The symbol of Shamash was a golden disc with a five—pointed star within and rays emitting from between the points. This is known as a *pentacle* or *pentagram*. When the pentagram has three sides down, it depicts *the female side* of Shamash called Shamesha and symbolizes *wisdom*. This is also a symbol of the goat of Mendes, which is the universal symbol for satanic worship, witchcraft and cults. The goat of Mendes is *androgynous* as is Shamesh. Androgynous is defined as having both masculine and feminine characteristics in one, being neither distinguishably male nor female in dress, appearance or behavior. Therefore, the *spirit of conflict* is the power behind the confusion and war of *gender identity* and *sexual orientation* that rages within the souls of humanity.

When the pentagram is shown with two sides down it depicts the male side of Shamash and symbolized *discipline, law and order*. This is seen as the sheriffs' star of today. The pentagram is comprised of a circle which depicts the feminine and a five pointed star that depicts the masculine that enforces through violence or the threat of violence, the wish of the feminine attribute. This takes us back to pagan goddess worship, as the pentagram has long been the symbolic representation of mother Earth. The five points of the star in relation to Mother Earth represents the four elements of nature and the fifth point represents the spirit realm. This combination of the circle and star is supposed to invoke the earths' energy force.

Speaking prophetically, the earth represents mankind, especially the carnal nature of man. Thus, the spirit of conflict evokes the bestial and primal nature of man. The manifestation of mans' carnal depravity causes confusion and leads to war and other acts of barbarism. James 3:16 says it best, "where envying and strife (conflict) is, there is confusion and *every* evil work."

Thrones of Power

Amraphel, King of Shinar

Amraphels' name means *keeper of the gods and one that speaks of dark things.* This indicates that this king was a *practitioner* or even a *priest* of mystical arts and demonic gods. It also implies that he served as a channel or medium for demonic spirits to speak through. Amraphel would then need to not only be *in communication* with these spirits, but also be totally given over to and possessed by them. Thus, demonic counsel influenced all of his direction and decisions. *This is the spirit of divination.*

Divination is the unlawful gathering and dispensing of knowledge from forbidden sources. In Genesis the third chapter Eve's consumption of the fruit of the tree in the midst of the garden was an act of divination in that she gained knowledge illegally. King Saul participated in divination in I Samuel the twenty-eighth chapter when he inquired of the witch of Endor concerning his future. In both instances divination led to devastation and ruin.

Amraphel was king of Shinar. Shinar is the Jewish name for Babylon, which means *gate of the gods*. A gate is a device that controls passage, entrance and exit. It is something that gives access, an opening. Therefore, Babylon was a *gateway city* that served as *a portal for demonic entities to traffic* to and fro in the earth. Babylon believed in many gods and goddesses and so, had a great pantheon of deities. The natural god of the Babylonians was Marduk. Marduk is purported to have four eyes, four ears and flames emitting from his mouth whenever he speaks. He was in control of *the four winds*, was believed to have granted Babylon as a home for the gods and was said to have created humans to work for and be slaves for the gods.

The attributes of Marduk are significant in that "wind" represents *spirit* and "home" represents *a place of abode* and "slaves" indicate *bondage*. Therefore, because of the multiplicity of demonic spirits that resided or lived not only in the geographical area of Babylon but also in the souls of the people, the nationals were in great bondage. One of the most important gods of the Babylonian pantheon is Enlil or Bel, god of the atmosphere, wind, storm and bad weather. *Enlil was considered the most active god in the pantheon.* Enlil is translated as Lord of the Air. His center of worship was at Nippur, also a part of modern day Iraq. Enlil was also the demon god purported to give kings their positions and give them success in war and peace. He is known as a strong, powerful and merciless god.

Because of the great numbers and diversity of demon spirits worshipped the foundation of power behind the throne of Amraphel is religion. Religion amasses wealth through the devotion and sacrifices of its followers. It was this source of wealth that supported the throne and reign of Amraphel. The Giving Foundation estimated that in the year 2005, 93.18 billion dollars occurred in religious giving in the United States alone. While there is no dependable source that gathers statistics on international religious giving, USAID estimates it at an extremely conservative 5.4 billion dollars. Religion motivates its initiates to give out of fear in order to appease an angry god or to keep him from becoming angry and doling out cruel punishment. True giving, however, is inspired by love. "For God *so loved* the world, that he *gave*...." John 3:16.

Four Demon Kings

Ruling Principalities and their Base of Power

So far, we have four powerful demon kings and *ruling principalities* that were established and originated from Iran, Syria, Iraq and Babylon, (which is also included in modern day Iraq). These countries are in what is called "the hot bed" of the Middle East. Used in this context, a hot bed is defined as an environment conducive to rapid, vigorous growth and development, *especially of something bad*.

The first king is a demonic reaper or devouring spirit. The foundation of power or principality behind it is the occult. This power genders spirits of hopelessness, despair and failure as it raids the lives of people again and again leaving them with nothing. No matter how hard they try or how much they accomplish, it is *suddenly consumed* by the reaper.

As stated before, *the foundation of established power that supports this king is the occult*. The word occult means *to hide conceal or keep secret*. The acts of sexual perversion and incest that accompany and characterize this spirit are most often *not talked about*, especially by those who are victimized. Thus, the identity, sexual wholeness and self-worth of the victim are *constantly* being devoured. These acts become *"personal"* or *"family"* secrets that are carried for years as the occult establishes a base of power within that individual, their family and generations to come. The spirit of failure usually plagues these people.

This is the principality behind the permeation of sexual perversion in the earth, the world *(the systems that govern the earth)* and the church. Lust, fornication, adultery, pornography, pedophilia, pederasty, incest and any other sexual perversion are gendered by the occult.

Remember, the occult spirit conceals evil deeds. Consider the MSNBC August 2006 report of the pastor of a rural Ozarks church who, along with his wife and her two brothers, was accused of sexually molesting young girls within his congregation for a period of ten years. The pastor is reported to have told the girls "We are preparing your body for service to God." This unholy reaping of the precious fruit of innocence and trust is only one of many examples. Occult spirits aid in the concealment of the down-low husband who reaps the life of his wife through sexually transmitted AIDS acquired from his homosexual lover to the corporate businessperson who loses everything to the reaper because an employee has been embezzling company funds.

As mentioned before, in the sixth chapter of Judges, the Bible gives the account of Israel's suffering at the hands of the Midianites, Amalekites and other Eastern tribes who waited until Israel's crops were ripe, harvested and on the threshing floor before swooping down in a murderous raid, leaving them with nothing. This happened so often that Judges 6:6 states that it left the children of Israel "greatly impoverished." The word *impoverished* in Judges 6:6 is the Hebrew word *"dawlal"* and means to be weak, feeble, to bring low and to be emptied. The reaper leaves one in a state of despondency with little or no strength to fight. This spirit feeds off of the despair of nations. To despair is to be overcome by a sense of futility or defeat; it is something that destroys and leaves one with an utter lack of hope.

Thus, if an area has an *abnormally high incident* of sexual perversion and violation, failure to succeed, poverty, depression, infirmity (moral, mental or physical weakness) and despondency, the ruling power or king is a "reaper" or "devouring" spirit. The power or principality behind it is the occult.

The second king is a demonic fear. The foundation of power or principality behind it is witchcraft. This demon king releases *multiple phobias* or various spirits of fear upon the land. *Phobias are potentially detrimental* and can interfere with ones ability to work, socially interact and even with ones daily routine. Some phobias become an extreme disability as they cripple the lives of people on a daily basis. Phobias are emotional and physical reactions to feared objects, people or situations. If a thing or situation can be imagined or exist, the enemy assigns a spirit of fear to it.

"Anxiety disorders are the most common mental illness in the U.S., affecting 19.1 million adults between 18 and 54" (The Roanoker Magazine—January/February 2006). The Canadian Mental Health Association reports that "One in six Canadians is affected by an anxiety disorder" and France, according to NOP World Health, "has the highest proportion of patients suffering from anxiety." Phobias are considered an anxiety disorder. Anxiety is defined as a state of uneasiness and distress, apprehension, intense fear and dread. The word anxiety is derived from the Latin *anxius* and literally means "to torment." Hence, 1 John 4:18 "There is no fear in love; but perfect love casteth out fear: *because fear hath torment.* He that feareth is not made perfect in love."

Phobias are divided into categories. Agoraphobia is the fear of being alone in any place or situation from which it seems impossible or difficult to escape or where help is unavailable. Phobias in this category include but are not limited to fear of busy streets, crowded places and places where people gather. Agoraphobia is derived from two Greek words, *agora* meaning open spaces and *phobia* meaning fear. Thus, agoraphobia is literally the fear of open spaces and more specifically fear of the marketplace. Twice as common in women as in men agoraphobia is the most common type of phobia. Some agoraphobics are so crippled by fear that they will not even leave their homes.

Social Phobia is the fear of being watched or humiliated while doing something in front of others. This ranges from signing a check, eating or drinking and most commonly, speaking in public. Social phobia usually develops after puberty and becomes greatest after thirty. *Persons with social phobia do not like other people looking at them.* They become very uncomfortable, nervous, irritated and can be angered simply because they are being observed.

Specific Phobia is an irrational fear of specific objects or situations such as the fear of heights, closed spaces, dogs, snakes, light, water etc. Because there is no limit to things or situations than can be feared the list of phobias is endless. From ablutophobia—fear of washing or bathing, achluophobia—fear of darkness, androphobia—fear of men, brontophobia—fear of thunder and lightning, cacophobia—fear of ugliness, genophobia—fear of sex, gynephobia—fear of women, kaorrhapiophobia—fear of failure or defeat, melophobia—fear or hatred of music, obesophobia—fear of gaining weight, necrophobia—fear of death or dead things, arithmophobia—fear of math or numbers to phronemophobia—the fear of thinking, people are assailed and bound by waves of fear. It is through this fear that the enemy intimidates, manipulates and ultimately dominates the lives of the people. This is witchcraft. People are unduly influenced and their lives, gifts, resources and abilities are prostituted for the support and continuance of a demonic throne. *This is the spirit of exploitation.*

Luke 21:26 declares that *the hearts of men would fail them* because of fear. Fear is the opposite of faith and renders men weak, broken and insane. This king *must* be slaughtered because, *"God hath not given us the spirit of fear; but of power, and of love, and of a sound mind."* II Timothy 1:7 Therefore, if an area experiences *an abnormally high rate of heart failure, heart related disease, prostitution and exploitation* the ruling king is fear and the principality behind it is witchcraft.

The third king is a demon of war. Conflict is the foundation of power behind this monarch. Conflict is defined as a state of open fighting, disagreement and disharmony, to clash and collide. *Unresolved conflict inevitably erupts into full-fledged war.* Thus, the power or principality behind the throne creates and sustains mass conflict "in the earth" that *war* might manifest. When speaking of war *"in the earth"*, we speak of not only the geographic planet earth but also of *mankind* who is made from the earth. Therefore, conflict and war are found *within* the earth, (mankind), and *upon* the earth, (the planet). Warfare upon the earth costs billions in lives and dollars. Recurring war drains wealth, upsets markets and keeps economic growth down. War is expensive, destructive and disruptive. Its' cost can be counted in money, resources, capital, human lives, trade, resource avail-ability and labor.

Most wars are fought over control of territory. For instance, the possession of Jerusalem has been the source of war for many years. From the Philistines to the Assyrians, from Babylon to Greece and Rome, Syria, Lebanon, Egypt and more have all fought for control of Jerusalem. The HolyLand Network states that "The rulership of Jerusalem has changed hands some twenty-six times." Sometimes wars occur when opposing factions fight over a resource such as farmland, minerals, a seaport or oil. An example of this is found in Genesis 26:18-20 where we find the account of Isaac's herdsmen and the herdsmen of Gerar striving for con-trol of a well of water.

Governments finance wars in many ways; one general way is through taxation. As the enemy fights to control human destiny, he mercilessly taxes the faith, strength and resources of the people. His goal is to leave them in a state of utter des-titution. War *undermines* prosperity as it fuels inflation and causes the value of currency to drop. The casualties of war are horrendous but still do not compare to the measure of loss in terms of individual suffering. Psychiatric breakdown remains one of the most costly points of war today. Close range, interpersonal, aggressive confrontation is one of the main factors in psychiatric casualties. This can trigger anxi-ety, panic attacks, acute stress, bipolar disorder, depression, psychotic behavior and more. *These are the results of war caused by spirits of trauma and insanity.*

When in engaged in war, most humans stop thinking with the forebrain, the part that makes us human, and start thinking with the mid-brain. The mid-brain is the *primitive* portion of our brain which cannot be distinguished from that of an animal. Thus, the more humans are engaged in and exposed to war, the more bestial they become. As the bestial nature of man is evoked he becomes more aggressive and violent, becoming resistant to the *violence immune system.* This system exists in the mid-brain and keeps members of a species from killing their own kind. Thus, constant exposure to war and conflict weakens this immune system and increases the possibility of humankind committing homicide. War also opens the door for *the spirit of murder.* For, while all murder is homicide all homicides are not considered murder. The Law.com dictionary defines murder as the following: "the killing of a human being by a sane person, with intent, malice aforethought (prior intention to kill the particular victim or anyone who gets in the way) and with no legal excuse or authority."

The same spirits of trauma insanity and murder operate when war is waged *"within the earth."* If you recall, the goddess worship connected to the principality of conflict involved an *androgynous spirit.* This spirit could be both male and female in behavior, dress and characteristics without *distinguishing* one from the other. When there isn't any distinction there isn't any clarity. Where there is no clarity there is doubt and confusion. The Medline Plus Medical Dictionary by Merriam-Webster defines confusion as "disturbance of consciousness characterized by inability to engage in orderly thought or by lack of power to distinguish, choose, or act decisively". It is further defined in the Second College Edition American Heritage Dictionary as "an early stage of psychosis involving mental and emotional disturbances." Therefore, war brings about confusion.

Androgynous spirits cause *gender conflict*, a war of sexuality. Gender identity disorder describes a conflict between a person's physical or apparent gender and that which they feel themselves to be inside. For instance, a person identified as a boy may actually feel and act like a girl. People with gender identity disorder often feel that they were born in the wrong body. Identity issues can manifest in different ways and open the door for other disorders such as depression, anxiety, relationship difficulties, personality disorders and homosexuality. These disorders are usually compounded by demonic spirits that serve to fasten this type of behavior into a *fixed pattern* by establishing a stronghold in the mind and sexuality of the person.

Disorder is defined as a lack of order or regular arrangement, *confusion*, a breach of civic order or peace, public disturbance and an ailment that affects the *function* of mind or body. Hence, we see that war brings with it *spirits of disorder, dysfunction, discord* and once again confusion. The Apostle

Paul reminds us in I Corinthians 14:33 that confusion is not of God.

You may recall that the star or pentacle that served as a symbol of goddess worship represented wisdom and justice. It is quite evident that any wisdom or justice dispensed by war is perverted. "This wisdom descendeth not from above, but is earthly, sensual, devilish." James 3:15 "If thou seest the oppression of the poor and violent perverting of judgment and justice in a province, marvel not ..." (Ecclesiastes 5:8a). This is *the spirit of corruption.*

Transparency International is an international non-governmental organization that addresses corruption. They also publish an annual report called the Corruption Perception Index that collects data based on polls. The data is then used for "ordering the countries of the world according to 'the degree to which corruption is perceived to exist among public officials and politicians'" (Wikipedia Free Encyclopedia, CPI). The spirit of corruption enervates a country and its people. It is linked with and leads to poverty because it obstructs economic growth.

Thus, if an area experiences *high incidents of violence, murder, psychological problems, domestic violence, gender identity confusion and governmental corruption* the ruling king is war and the principality behind it is conflict. This prince is also known as *strife.*

The fourth king is divination. The principality or foundation of power behind this throne is religion. Divination is the occult practice of gaining information by illegal supernatural means. This practice has swept the globe in every form possible, from hepatoscopy, tarot cards, mirror scrying, crystal balls, runes and ouija boards to horoscopes. It is ancient and one of the most basic and frequently used forms of witchcraft. Babylonians considered divination a major intellectual achievement and most senior ariolaters were men of influence who were held in high esteem. Private individuals and heads of state consulted these ariloaters or diviners. Kings and Queens who sought consul frequently inquired of them.

Babylonians believed that the gods communicated their intentions through omens and signs. These included but were not limited to smoke, falling stars, the flocking of birds, eclipses and the position of the stars. They studied every movement especially those of the heavens. This was such a way of life that even the army was always accompanied by a diviner. In Ezekiel 21:21 King Nebuchadnezzar of Babylon stands at a fork in the road on his way to conquer Judah and decides through divination which way to proceed. *"For the king of Babylon stood at the parting of the way, at the head of the two ways, to use divination: he made his arrows bright, he consulted with images, he looked in the liver."* Hepatoscopy or looking into the liver is one of the most ancient forms of divination. This was because the liver was seen as the seat of life and passions.

Life and passion, the needs of both are fodder for the spirit of divination. Humans have an insatiable *need to know* what will happen in their lives and if they will obtain, sustain and maintain the object of their passions. It is this quest for unknown information that leads them into the snare of religion. Religion is defined as ceremonial ritualistic observance, to pursue with zeal and conscientious devotion and the belief in a supernatural power or powers. It is the ceremonial ritualistic observance coupled with zeal that gives religion its power and momentum.

Ceremonial rituals are simply a set of prescribed acts that are carried out with *strict adherence* during religious events. This means that things are done the same way over and over again with no room for growth or change. This practice is "handed down" from one generation to another, all the while building a stronghold of tradition. Tradition literally means, *to hand down*. Religion promotes the handing down of strict adherence to ritual while negating relationship and leaving the soul and spirit of man void of direction, guidance and assurance. This of course leads them back to divination.

Religion keeps man in a constant state of dissatisfaction as he reaches for the unattainable; seeks to know that which will never be divulged and delves into that which has been forbidden. It is the great whore of Babylon peddling her wares to all who are enticed. In the seventeenth chapter of Revelation the term "whore" is a metaphor used to designate the idolatry of Babylon, its inhabitants and leaders. Because Babylon was at one time a world power and exercised influence over other nations, it is stated, *"the inhabitants of the earth have been made drunk with the wine of her fornication."* This signifies the far-reaching effects of religion. Religion intoxicates humanity. Intoxicate means to stupefy, stimulate, excite and poison. The demonic king of divination ravages the soul of man as he reels in drunken religious stupor.

The chief deity of Babylon was Enlil or Bel, god of the atmosphere. Atmosphere is defined in several ways, however, the one that applies to Enlil is; *environment or surroundings that have psychological, physical or other influence.* The principality of religion sets the cultural climate of a region and its people. The religion of a people decides the standards of behavior and acceptable lifestyle and also determines the veneration of some and the degradation of others. Thus, if religion sets the cultural climate, it also the moral values of men.

When Babylon permanently became the political center of the region, Marduk became the chief deity and absorbed the powers of Enlil and the other gods. Marduk was said to spit fire when he spoke, to be a god of magic, wisdom and war *and* to command the four winds of the earth. Prophetically wind represents spirit. There are four kings, four principalities and four winds. The four winds are the plethora of demonic companies; division, rank and file, which are assigned to and sent out by the four kings. Religion acts as the lord of hosts and is actually the *chief principality* of them all!! Religion comes from the Latin word religare; *re* meaning "to return" and *ligare* meaning "to bind." Thus, religions' sole purpose is to bring mankind back into a state of bondage through religious obligation.

Zechariah 5:5–11 tells of wickedness building a house and establishing a base in Shinar. Shinar is the Hebrew name for Babylon. I believe the wickedness spoken of is the governing principality of religion. It has spread from its base to the four corners of the earth. The present day nations of the four kings; Iraq, Iran and Syria are a hot bed of religious conflict that affects the rest of the world politically and economically.

Hence, if there are abnormally high legalistic ceremonial ritualistic codes imposed through religious institutions that do not allow for relationship, growth and change and if the people of the region seek after diviners in great numbers, the king of that region is divination and the founding power or principality is religion. It is through divination or *false prophecy* that the throne is funded as people yield their treasure to the great whore.

Religion is a deadly counterfeit. It was luciferically designed to replace the intimate relationship and communion between God and man. Religion makes man seem pious through his faithful adherence to ritual even though he never changes or grows in behavior and character. His spirit remains wicked, his passions perverse, his thoughts outrageous and his actions ungodly. *"Hath God said?"* is the man-tra of the masses. This is the effect of religion upon and in the earth.

RELIGION

Manifestations

Religion has nothing to do with God even though you will find it deeply entrenched in churches, temples, mosques, synagogues and the lives of those who profess to be the *"people of God."* Religion substitutes religious activity for the power of the Holy Spirit and true relationship with God. It also breeds spirits of *religious arrogance* and *religious pride*.

Religious arrogance causes one to feel superior to others because they are faithful in adhering to the rituals of their faith such as praying or fasting. Religious pride causes one to feel exalted about the works they do such as outreach and charitable acts. This is an unholy trinity: religion, religious arrogance and religious pride. These demons empower the spirit of sectarianism. Sectarianism occurs when members of a larger group cut themselves off and divide. This usually occurs because of heresy. Heresy is a controversial or unorthodox opinion that varies from and opposes established religious beliefs. Sectarianism leads to denominationalism. Denominationalism is defined as the tendency to separate. Thus, religion causes separation, discrimination and division.

Religion also causes those bound by it to be institutionalized. To be institutionalized is to *take on the character* of an institute. An institution is a custom or behavioral pattern of importance in the life of a community or society. Therefore, religious institutions impress upon its' followers the character and personality *of the institute* rather than that of God. Because of this individual personalities are swallowed up and suppressed. Everyone talks, walks, acts and dresses the same. This is religious colonization at its worse.

Religion is a governing principality that interfaces itself with a system and becomes an integral part of its makeup. To *govern* means to make and administer the *public policy* and affairs, to exercise sovereign authority, *to control*, keep under control, regulate and restrain. A policy is a plan or course of action. Hence, religions' purpose is to control the actions of the people. That is why it interfaces with the *political systems* of the world. Communism, Socialism and The Third Reich are all examples of political religious systems.

Religion is a seduction of the mind. To seduce is to entice or beguile into a desired state or position. It literally means to lead away. Religion leads mankind *away* from God. Matthew 23: 15 reads as follows: "Woe unto you, scribes and Pharisees, hypocrites! For ye compass sea and land to make one proselyte (convert), and when he is made, ye make him two fold more the child of hell than yourselves." Thus, religious spirits perpetuate themselves and do not convert men to the Lord, but rather present a distorted image of God.

Distortion is defined as giving a false or misleading account of; to misrepresent. Religion misrepresents God. *Because religion is occult in nature it is riddled with secrets and lies.* The word "occult" comes from the Latin *occulere* and means to conceal, hide or keep secret. As stated previously, religion impresses upon the devotee the character of the institution and not that of God. Therefore, religious institutions are filled with religious people of ungodly character. It is this ungodly character that promotes secret sins or iniquity. *Iniquity is that which is perverse and wicked.* Perverse means to be twisted, crooked and abnormal. The word wicked means to be injurious in effect, detrimental, causing suffering, damage and pain. Thus, *religion causes people to outwardly seem chaste and pious while secretly participating in the debauchery of perverse wickedness or twisted pain.* Religion shackles mankind with pleasurable torment, tearing and twisting the soul until the image of God is destroyed. This is the ultimate purpose of religion; *to destroy the image of God in mankind and render him unusable.*

PREVAILING WINDS

The wind that blows most often across an area or region is the prevailing wind. The confederacy of the four demon kings assign spirits to specific geographical locations. Each locale will have "prevailing winds"; recurrent events that are particular to that region. It is important to note that it is prophetically significant that there are four kings. Four represents the four corners and the four winds of the earth signifying global rule. The four corners of the earth are North East West and South, the first letter of each word making the acronym NEWS. News is the events and happenings that occur in the world. You will find in every corner of the world that the spirits these kings represent are actively manifesting and causing events to occur in every strata of society. In both the Old and New Testament the word *spirit* is translated as "wind." Thus, a brief understanding of wind and how it operates will give us insight as to how these demon spirits affect the earth.

Wind is the natural movement of air. Air is a colorless, odorless gaseous mixture that moves through an enclosed atmosphere. Air attempts to flow from areas of high pressure to areas of low pressure. This movement creates air pressure. Air pressure is the pressure exerted by the weight of air over an area of the earths' surface. *Heated air causes an increase in pressure* because the air molecules are moving more rapidly and colliding into one another. Molecules move less rapidly in cooled air and *decrease* air pressure.

Air pressure is affected by altitude as well as ground conditions that differ from place to place. It is important to know that *air molecules are constantly bombarding us* from all directions, exerting constant pressure. The reason you cannot feel the air pressure exerted upon you is because *the air pressure within your body* balances that on the outside. The only way you can notice air pressure is if it changes rapidly such as when you ascend or descend. Hence, we are given to understand that we are being *persistently assailed* by demon spirits and that we are affected by it when either we change position and or allow the waning of the Holy Spirit in our lives. If we ascend and gain strength, the pressure will increase. However, *the anointing within our lives* should also increase to offset it. If we descend and grow weak, the pressure increases and intensifies until we allow the Holy Spirit to restore refresh and revive us.

There are different kinds of winds. *Global winds are currents that circulate around the earth* such as trade winds. These are winds that blow throughout the tropics, circulating air between the equator 30 degrees latitude north and south. Also included are Westerlies—winds traveling from the southwest to the nor east Polar Regions and Polar Easterlies—cold winds that blow from the northeast across the Polar Regions to the southwest. These represent spirits that have global impact as they move from place to place affecting nations with *common maladies* such as disease, discontent, poverty, social unrest, crime, unemployment, injustice, discrimination and so forth.

There are also winds called "local winds." Local winds are known as mesoscale or *regional* winds. These are winds that *blow across areas of the surface* ranging from a few miles to a hundred miles in width. A local wind can last from several minutes to several days. Local winds exist at various points around the world. Two main categories of local winds are sea breezes and land breezes. A sea breeze *blows from water to shore* and form on hot days when the temperature of the land warms more rapidly. Sea breezes are strongest at mid afternoon when the land reaches its maximum temperature. The strongest sea breezes blow in from the ocean.

Land breezes blow from the shore toward the water as the land cools. These types of winds occur in the evening and at night. From this we see that spirits are assigned to locales and regions and that there are specific times of the day and conditions when they are more active. Other local winds are levanters, chinooks, monsoons, derecho, dust devil, whirly, kona and so on. These winds vary in speed and intensity depending upon their locale.

Various numerous local winds are purported to be responsible for declines in the mental and physical condition of a regions inhabitants. For instance, the Chinook, a dry, warm katabatic wind that blows down the eastern side of the Rocky Mts., from New Mexico to Canada in winter or early spring, *is said to cause crabbiness, depression and illness.*

The Sirocco is a hot dry dusty, southeasterly wind out of North Africa that travels across the Mediterranean Sea. *It is said to cause laziness and mental illness.* Another wind is the Santa Anas that is said to make people *nervous, anxiety ridden and homicidal.* This is a warm dry wind that blows through southern California.

The last local wind we will explore is the Foehn, (pronounced fane). This is a warm and dry katabatic wind similar to a Chinook. The foehn flows down from the Alps onto the plains of Austria and Germany. It is said to drive people to commit suicide. Wealden Natural Health cites the article "Winds of Depression" as follows: "The Swiss Meteorological Institute made extensive studies into the problems arising from their local wind, the Foehn and in 1974 published a list of physical and mental effects it was found to cause. This list was extensive and included: body pains, sick headaches, dizziness, nausea, variations in body salts—sodium, calcium, magnesium, respiratory problems, asthma, higher incident of heart attacks, slower reaction time" and more.

Scientists wanted to know what was so different about the air in these winds that would cause them to have such effects. With many national and international organizations joining in the research, they discovered that the electrical charge which the wind carries in the form of ions was the culprit. An ion is an atom or a molecule, (which consists of two or more atoms that are bonded together), that, carries an electrical charge. This charge can be either positive or negative.

Ions are not just "in" the air but are actually a part of what air is because air is comprised of a mixture of gases which in turn are made of atoms. So it is in the spiritual realm, there are good spirits and evil spirits, godly and demonic; some acting in your favor while others seek to ultimately annihilate you. All of this reflects the influence of demonic spirits upon the people of the earth as they manifest in and through the worlds' systems. Therefore, the slaughter of the kings *must* occur so that the prevailing winds of our regions will be favorable.

STORM WINDS

Storms are large scale weather systems centered around an area of low atmospheric pressure, drawing in *contrasting* warm and cold fronts. They produce wind, clouds, precipitation and other types of unsettled weather. Weather is defined as the state of the atmosphere at a given time and place. The atmosphere is scientifically defined as the gaseous envelope that surrounds a celestial body. This definition alone has great spiritual implications; however, it is the following one that we will focus on: *atmosphere—the predominate tone or mood that is set in a place.*

Storm systems are centered around areas of low atmospheric pressure and draw or attract contrasting winds. Thus, areas or regions where the presence of God is minimal, and representatives of His kingdom are few or inactive, are plagued by violent spiritual storms as contrasting spirits clash and fight for control of the region and the souls within. This is what occurred in the four king conspiracy, these kings banded together to fight against other territorial nations who also wanted dominance. These nations were fierce in their own right and virtually unconquerable. If Chedorlaomer and the other kings had not banded together they would have most certainly met defeat. Let's take a look at some of these other opposing nations which we shall call "contrasting fronts."

The Rephaims in Ashteroth Karnaim were a race of giants and so were the Zuzims in Ham as well as the Emims in Shaveh Kiriatham. The Horites in Mt Seir were *troglodytes*, brutish in nature, cruel and savage. The Amelikites of Kadesh were a strong and mighty nomadic people. The Amorites in Hazezon—tamar, *descendants of Emor, fourth son of Canaan* were mountaineers of gargantuan size and strength. Thus, Chedolaomer and his confederacy defeated some of the fiercest warriors in the region in order to establish themselves as the conquering power.

As it was then, so is it today; as the spiritual atmosphere of the church disintegrates and spiritual storm systems form, contrasting spirits are attracted and begin to manifest in the Body of Christ. Contrast is defined as *to set in opposition in order to show the differences.* Contrast comes from the Latin *contravenire* which means to stand against! The hearts and spirits of Christians are waxing cold and beginning to "stand against" God. Yes, they are still going to and participating in church; rending their garments and not their heart. Chedolaomer, the demonic reaper, and the other foul kings are riding full tilt through the church, harvesting souls to stand against God. Many have been harvested and don't even know it as they have not examined themselves to see if they still be in the faith. Entire regions have succumbed to this campaign of conquest and are now manifesting the results of these prevailing winds. Something must be done! Is there not a champion king, a wind strong enough to defeat the spirits of darkness?? Chedolaomer and his demonic confederacy must be stopped! The land must be saved!

Alas, those that *could* help won't help. Minding their own business while basking nonchalantly in the security of apathy, those with authority, power and the means to effect powerful deliverance that will deliver the souls of men and restore the land choose to ignore the crisis or at best watch from afar. *How do we stir these placid winds?* If you recall, air molecules move more rapidly and collide with one another when the air is heated. Heated air also creates intense pressure. Thus, it seems something will have to occur that will *"turn up the heat"* in order to galvanize the stalwart warriors of righteousness.

The Taking of Lot
Removing the Veil

Lot, whose name means *veil* or *covering,* was Abrams nephew. Abram was a mighty man, a rich man and a man of God. While Chedolaomer ravaged the country there is no record that Abram did *anything* until Lot was taken captive. Lot's name means veil. A veil is defined as a piece of cloth, often transparent, worn over the head, shoulders and face. All three of these parts of the body have prophetic significance. *The head represents knowledge and authority, the shoulders government and responsibility and the face represents open confrontation.* As mentioned before, Abram is an apostolic type. Lot represents the veil that covers the apostolic function of the church. While there are those who recognize and function in apostolic fullness, the church as a whole is veiled. This veiling did not occur forcefully or unknowingly but was done through casual neglect. Let's revisit Genesis:

Genesis 12:1 "Now the LORD had said unto Abram, Get thee out of thy country, and from thy kindred, and from thy father's house, unto a land that I will shew thee:"

Gen 12:4 "So Abram departed, as the LORD had spoken unto him; *and Lot went with him*: and Abram was seventy and five years old when he departed out of Haran."

Abram was instructed to get out of his country and away from his kindred, but Lot went with him. This was in *direct disregard* to the instruction of the Lord and resulted in unnecessary infighting and strife (See Genesis 13:5—10). No doubt Abram did not think that taking Lot with him would cause any trouble or that it would displease the Lord. It was an allowance of something that God had disallowed, a dangerous disregard. It is this spirit of carnal and demonic disregard that is immobilizing the apostolic function of the church.

The word disregard means to neglect and pay no attention to. The church has been making certain allowances in *total disregard* to the Word and will of God. She has veiled herself thoroughly so that she can see no evil; acting as if it doesn't exist and therefore not have to acknowledge or act in authority against it. The church is veiled to hear no evil and thus is not responsible for giving sound counsel, instruction and guidance. And finally, she is veiled to speak no evil, hence avoiding any open confrontation that requires the imprecation of ungodliness. This is alarming since the church is the only power in the earth that *can* defeat the adversary and was birthed for just that purpose! Luke 10:19

Lot also represents kith and kindred, those that are near and dear to us. Sadly, it is only when the enemy threatens that which is ours do we break free from the stupor of nonchalance. When Abram heard that Lot was taken he armed his trained servants which had been born and raised in his own house. One of the apostolic functions of the church is to "train servants." To train is to make proficient with specialized instruction and practice; to prepare. The church is supposed to raise up servants who are efficiently prepared for any and all inevitability. Once sufficiently trained and proven they are to be armed, given authority to use the tools and weaponry that they have mastered through training. Abram took his trained servants and pursued the enemy in order to retake that which was precious to him.

In Genesis 14:14 Abram pursued the enemy to Dan. The name Dan means *judge*. The apostolic anointing has the authority to execute judgment upon the enemy. This is the ability to astutely evaluate the state of events which have occurred and draw sound conclusions. The Hebrew word most often used meaning "to judge" is *shaphat*, to pronounce sentence. This entails deciding what punishment is to be inflicted. In 1 Corinthians 6:3 the Apostle Paul poses this query: "Know ye not that we shall judge angels? how much more things that pertain to this life?" It is imperative that the apostolic function of the church become fully operative in its divine judicial authority in order to curtail the rampant havoc of the enemy.

Thus, Abram prevailed against and pursued the enemy to Hobah, which means *hiding place*. This is significant in that many times it seems that the enemy has been defeated and thoroughly routed only to discover that he has gone into hiding. The enemy uses this period of concealment to recover, regroup and re-strategize. Exercising patience, the enemy waits until the Church is lulled into a false sense of security to strike without warning at the most unexpected time in the most unexpected place. Therefore, it is essential that the warriors of Christ diligently identify and eradicate any possible place of demonic concealment. Remember, the apostolic anointing has the power to drive the enemy out of hiding, defeat him and return triumphantly with the spoils of victory!

Abram had the ability to defeat these four kings all along, *yet he did nothing* until Lot was taken. The veil of complacency is being lifted from the church as Lot is taken. Lot represents our children, communities, schools, jobs, homes and moral values. The enemy is getting too close for blind comfort as he brazenly encroaches into our personal domain. The apostolic function of the church is being galvanized as the Abrams of our day emerge from their spiritual catatonic state and become aware of the enemy's murderous rampage. These four demon kings and their hordes must be stopped and only the church operating in the full apostolic power of

God can do it! *"Wherefore he saith, Awake thou that sleepest, and arise from the dead, and Christ shall give thee light."* Ephesians 5:14

THE SLAUGHTER OF THE KINGS

Apostolic Retrieval

Abram defeated what was, *up until that time,* undefeatable. God has so empowered the church to destroy the destroyer. The spirits that these four kings represent have regrouped and reasserted themselves with extreme aggression because the apostolic function has been greatly ignored. However, the patriarchal anointing of the apostle has the ability to cover or protect the earth from the plague of demonic infestation.

Keep in mind, Chedolaomer and his confederates were giant killers. It is indeed a great feat to kill a giant and an even greater one to defeat the giant killer! Abram defeated the killer of giants, he conquered the conqueror! Through the Christ of God we become more than conquerors; the apostolic function operates in a dimension of warfare that slaughters demonic kings and demolishes thrones of iniquity, thus, bringing about multidimensional emancipation to various regions and their inhabitants.

Apostolic retrieval is a direct result of divine emancipation. It is the apostolic anointing that affects the return of all that was lost. Genesis 14:16 states that Abram brought back ALL; all includes the goods and the kindred. The Hebrew word for goods in Genesis 14:16 is *r'kush* and means *property*. The word property is defined as that which is owned or possessed by an individual. *Thus, the apostolic anointing has within it restorative ability to reinstate to the people of God that which was captured by the enemy.* This is the hour of apostolic retrieval as God begins to restore loved ones, homes and goods that have been held captive by the adversary.

In order to better understand the depths of what apostolic retrieval entails it will be helpful to gain a greater meaning of the word retrieve. Retrieve is defined as to *recover, regain and rescue.* To recover is to get back, to grow well and to obtain in return for injury or debt. *Thus, apostolic retrieval institutes healing and compensation in order to repair the damage inflicted through traumatic loss.* Regain is defined as to reach again; to once again possess the advantage, realize a profit and achieve progress; to arrive. Apostolic retrieval restores one to their *rightful position* in every area. To retrieve is also defined as to rescue; to save from hurt, harm, injury or danger. The apostolic anointing brings about deliverance; pulling and *keeping* from jeopardy.

Therefore, the slaughter of the kings *must* occur so that the mothers, fathers, sons and daughters, preachers, teachers, prophets and leaders, psalmists, writers, financiers and entertainers, inventors and healers and every soul that has been mercilessly taken by the enemy is retrieved! This will only happen when Abram, the apostolic function of the church, rises to the challenge with fully trained servants to pursue and overtake the enemy. Without Abram the land would have had no champion and without the church operating in apostolic authority the nations of the world do not either. It seems that we have been docilely waiting on God to bring everything back and God is waiting on us!

In I Samuel 30th chapter, David experiences something similar to Abram in that while he was away at war, the Amalekites swooped in and raided Ziklag, the home of David, his army and their families at the time. The Amalekites, (reapers), burned the city with fire and took the women and children captive. David and his army were devastated.

"And David enquired at the Lord, saying, Shall I pursue after this troop? Shall I overtake them? And he answered him, Pursue: for thou shalt surely overtake them and without fail recover all" (I Samuel 30:8). Just like David, the cry of the church is the same: Shall we pursue? Shall we overtake them? God is waiting for the church to shake herself from the grief of devasta-

tion. David's loss was great, the feelings of guilt overwhelming, nevertheless, he knew things were not going to change unless he did something about it. He was not willing to allow the enemy to have his family, his goods, nor the victory! Neither was he willing to tolerate the wholesale scavenging of those who had been faithful in battle, to God and to him. David in essence told God *"I will not stand for this! I am a warrior, it's what I do and I am ready to vindicate this vile offense against the name and people of God! All I need to know from you is do I have your permission and are you with me??!!"*

God is waiting for the church to rise in righteous indignation as the people of God are dragged away captive by the demon kings of consumption, (the reaper), fear, war and divination. For the spirit of the Lord gives the same answer; pursue! To pursue means to chase with *hostile* intent. "For, we wrestle not against flesh and blood, but against principalities, against powers, against the rulers of the darkness of this world, against spiritual wickedness in high places." Ephesians 6:12

The sword of the Lord is whetted as the day of apostolic retrieval dawns. The apostolic generals are stirring, the hand of God in the earth, (the five—fold ministry), is beginning to unfold and stretch out as the power of the apostle touches each finger and anoints them for battle! For, surely, as the Body of Christ arises to take a stand against the adversary, the hand of God will take up the sword of the spirit therewith to slaughter the kings. "For the weapons of our warfare are not carnal, but mighty through God ..." (II Corinthians 10: 4).

In I Samuel 30:8 God gives David this assurance; *"for thou shalt surely overtake them, and without fail recover all."* The goods and the kindred that have been taken by the enemy will be recovered without fail!! It doesn't matter what king has them, they will be recovered without fail! *Without fail!!* That is the cry of the apostolic army of the Lord; "WITH-OUT FAIL!" Therefore, expect to experience the manifestation of apostolic retrieval as the church returns victoriously triumphant from the slaughter of the kings!

Four

A Significant Number

In the theology of numerology four has great significance in that on the fourth day of creation God set the established order for spiritual authority. Genesis 1:14 states, that God placed lights in the firmament of the heaven to divide the day from the night. The word *lights* in this passage of scripture means luminaries. A luminary is a leading light, so called because of its ability to bring one into correct understanding of the truth; illumination. *Therefore, these lights were placed in the firmament or expanse of the heaven to help one to properly discern the difference between darkness and light.* The firmament in this scripture, while actually referring to the sky, is also a prophetic metaphor for the spiritual realm as well as the mind.

God further states that the luminaries or lights shall be for *signs, seasons, days* and *years*. Signs are used to indicate that which is or that which is to come, therefore, the luminaries mark current and coming events. A season is an opportune period of time when specific events are most favorable to occur. Thus, the luminaries indicate right timing. (Farmers refer to almanacs which inform them when and what to plant based on the luminaries). The luminaries not only mark the passing of days and years but can often indicate what *kind* of day or year it will be.

In Genesis 1:15, God states that *the purpose of the lights* in the firmament of the heavens is to give light to the earth. The word earth prophetically signifies humanity as a whole. Therefore, the luminaries were purposefully created and positioned to give mankind guidance, discernment and the correct understanding of the truth. What are these luminaries of the spirit that God has so entrusted to give light to man?

Genesis 1:16 says that God made two great lights. The word *great* in this scripture means mighty; having great power or ability to act, a strong force. It is imperative to note that *both lights* are made "great" by God. The greater light is the Sun, which prophetically represents Jesus the Christ of God. It is to rule the day, that which is light, life and good. The lesser light is, of course, the Moon, which prophetically represents the church, and is to rule the night; darkness, death and evil. The word *rule* is defined as to *govern* which is to *dominate, exercise power and authority*. The moon naturally has no light of its own, but rather reflects the light of the sun into the darkness. Hence, the church has been given power and authority by God through his son Jesus to dominate the satanic powers of darkness, death and all that is evil!

After making the two great lights, God made the stars. Stars prophetically represent angels; deputy messengers. These angels are divinely created supernatural beings as well as men and women who are especially anointed and set aside as messengers of God. The Hebrew word for angel, *malak,* also means deputy and indicates one who is empowered with authority to enforce the government of God. Thus, these two great lights; Christ and his church, along with the stars; the angels of Heaven *and* Earth are "set" in the firmament of the heaven or the spirit realm in order to govern; establish and maintain order. Thus, four is the number that establishes spiritual order.

In an adversatively brazen attempt to overturn the spiritual authority and order of God, the enemy has released and sanctioned four chief principalities, four primary kings and four demonic river winds. Rivers represent life force; the essential needed to maintain, sustain and carry out a plan, plot or scheme. The life force of the four kings is the river of numerous demonic hordes that enact the insidious conspiracy of Satan. These are spirits that have been let loose into the earth to capture the souls of men.

Also note that the four kings came from four city states of a particular region; Elam, Aram, Ellasar and Shinar. These four city states make up modern day Iran, Syria and Iraq. It is here, in this region of the earth that archeologists of the mid—nineteenth century have proclaimed the cradle of civilization. The cradle of civilization refers to mankind's development of stationary agrarian societies. While both India and Kenya have been purported to be cradles of civilization it must be noted that some of the oldest known recorded history has been excavated in the Middle East.

On the other hand, Africa is touted as the place of mankind's origination. Could it be possible that these two; ancient Africa and ancient Mesopotamia are connected? One theory that could support this proposition is that of Pangaea; the supercontinent that existed before the earth separated into the continents of today. Upon observing maps and satellite imagery of Africa and the Middle East it readily appears that these two areas were once connected.

Genesis 2:15 states "And the LORD God took the man, and put him into the garden of Eden to dress it and to keep it." Two key words here are "took" and "put". This implies that man was possibly created in one location and later placed in the Garden of Eden. Genesis 2: 8—14 gives a brief geographical sketch of the Garden of Eden. It states that one river or life source parted into four in order to water the garden. Two of those rivers are known today as the Euphrates and the Tigris which flow from the mountains of Turkey and run through Iraq. The other two rivers were the Gihon and the Pishon. The Gihon is considered to be the Abay

River of today that runs through Ethiopia and forms the upper part of the Blue Nile. The Pishon has not been located. Even though the topography of the land has changed, in light of the Pangaea theory this would suggest that the Garden of Eden was in ancient Mesopotamia which is now comprised of modern day Iraq, eastern Syria, southeastern Turkey and southwest Iran. Therefore, it is quite possible that the cradle of humanity or origin of mankind was in Africa and that the location of the Garden of Eden was in the Middle East.

Therefore, it is my belief that the Middle East is a portal or gateway by which dominion of the earth is realized. For, if the scholars and archeologists are correct, then it is here that dominion over the earth was first given to man, it is here that dominion was lost and it is here that it was regained. *"And a river went out of Eden to water the garden; and from thence it was parted, and became into four heads."* (Genesis 2:10) Satan's desire is to control the river, or spiritual life force, that affects the growth and development of humanity.

The Middle East is also the place where the three main continents of the Old World meet; Europe, Africa and Asia. Those that would be world conquerors *knew* that they would have to pass through this region in order to expand their domain. Thus, it is from here that the unholy trinity of four, breach the gate and pour into the four corners of the earth. And, while there is unrest in other areas of the world, nowhere is it as constant and volatile as the Middle East.

The Fourth Watch

Jesus Walks

Jews divided a twenty four hour period into three parts of four hours each called watches. However, the Romans, *under whose rule they were*, divided a twenty four hour period into four parts of three hours each. Thus, the period between 3:00 a.m. and 6:00 a.m. is called the fourth watch.

The fourth watch is the time when there is the most spiritual activity; remember, four is the number that denotes the assertion and establishment of spiritual authority and order. It is during this watch that conflict over supremacy of a human life is the greatest. For, while many sleep, demonic spirits seek inroads to capture their soul and assert the spiritual disorder of Satan instead of the divine order of God.

Nevertheless, someone is watching. "And in the fourth watch of the night Jesus went unto them walking on the sea"

(Matthew 14:25). Previous to this Jesus had compelled his disciples to get into a ship and cross over the sea to the other side. While doing so, the disciples encountered a violent storm with contrary winds. Mark 6:48 states that they were toiling or *tormented* in their rowing. The prophetic significance of this is that the ship represents the church and the disciples are those within it. The sea represents the spirit realm as well as multitudes of people. The contrary winds are demonic spirits and the storm is the manifestation of the warfare and atmospheric disturbance they wage.

It was in the midst of this chaos, when the ship was being tossed to and fro, that Jesus came unto them walking on the sea. *To walk on something denotes the exercising of dominion and authority over it.* Jesus sees the church being tormented in her rowing, tossed to and fro by waves of disturbed people who are influenced by contrary winds and thus attempting to thwart the churches ability to progress and expand the Kingdom of God.

The divine order of God must be exerted in the church as leadership and laity alike are embroiled in bitter scandal leaving the masses with tarnished faith and listless despondency. *Jesus walks the fourth watch!!* The Bible states that when he came into the ship the winds ceased. He could have dispersed the demonic powers before even approaching the ship, however, this is a prophetic lesson; without Christ in it the church is powerless.

Even as he reassured his disciples then and restored their faith by causing the contrary winds to cease tossing the ship, he walks now, as the Chief Apostle, to strengthen the church, renew faith and restore spiritual order! There may be four chief principalities. There may be four primary kings and there may be four major river winds. And, this may seem to be the season of their greatest manifestation. But, *this is also the fourth watch....* Jesus walks!! He is manifesting his apostolic authority in the earth and the spirit realm *through* the church! So, rise up! Put on your armor and take up your weapons! Set yourselves in array! Pursue, overtake and recover all *without fail!* For, once again, it is time ... *for the slaughter of the kings!*

Contact Information

Dr. *Anya M. Hall*
SENIOR APOSTLE
I CORINTHIANS 3:10A
"A Wise Master Builder"

"The tektonic plates of the earth are always in motion, therefore, the next shift you will experience is your imminent move into destiny!"

www.tektonministries.com

1-866-95-SHIFT

P.O. Box 690786
Orlando, Fl 32869
apostle@tektonministries.com

Executive Administrator
Valamere Mikler
divinecalling_1@hotmail.com
407 - 996 - 6971

JESUSINORLANDO.COM PRESENTS

The Master Builder Show

with Apostle Anya Hall

every week / Track #2 ONLY on

DISCERNING YOUR SEASON BY XULON PRESS
AVAILABLE WHEREVER BOOKS ARE SOLD!
ORDER YOURS TODAY!!

This two CD set of five minute devotions is designed to speak to various issues of life and help you to achieve healing, deliverance and freedom.Listen to one each day and receive encouragement and strength. Remember, the Word of God is meant to be experienced. Order yours today!

www.tektonministries.com or email *apostle@tektonministries.com*

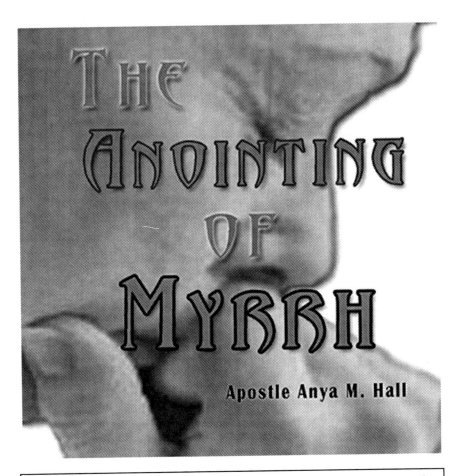

"*Destroying Spirits of Religious Tradition!*"

Anya M. Hall

TEACH MY HANDS TO WAR

Based on Psalms 144:1, Teach My Hands to War teaches the believer the fundamentals of spiritual warfare!! This book gives prophetic insight into the three main weapons of Christians: The Blood, The Word and The Name of Jesus!! The time for a weapons upgrade is NOW!!
Order yours today!! www.tektonministries.com

POSSESSING THE GATE!!
WHOEVER CONTROLS THE GATE HOLDS THE POWER!!

This powerful book apostolically defines gates, keys and access! It also gives tactical wisdom for spiritual reconnaissance and strong admonition on how to defeat demonic gatekeepers! This is a **MUST HAVE** for every progressive and serious Kingdom Builder!

The **8th Day** is a powerful apostolic and prophetic teaching concerning the new age that the church and the world at large has shifted into. This four CD set begins with *"Pharaoh's Dream"* which prophetically warns of an economic famine that can only be offset by the wisdom of God during days of divine prosperity. Each succeeding CD delves deeper into the future revealing government cover ups, demonic trafficking, divine intervention and much much more!! Purchase the entire set and receive the **8th day journal** complete with *prophetic phat tips*!

PEOPLE OF WAR

God needs a people who will rise, stand and fight! He desires a people who will set their cities on fire for the Lord through revival, fasting and prayer. Tragically, it seems as if the warriors of the Lord are suffering from spiritual fatigue and extreme exhaustion. *This is a deadly condition that must be remedied!* Find out how in The People of War.

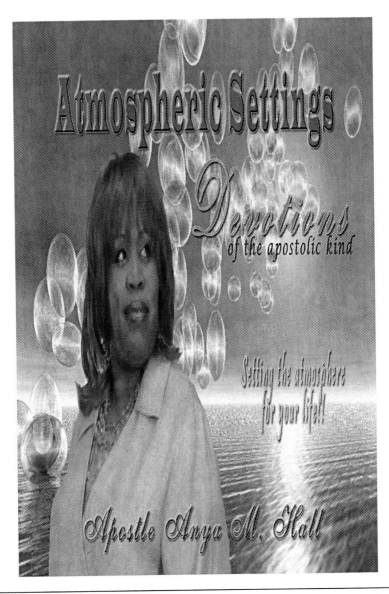

This is a must have devotional tool that will bring peace, comfort and strength to you and set the atmosphere for your life! Log on to www.tektonministries.com

Bibliography

Reference Materials

The American Heritage Dictionary, 2nd College Edition, Copyright © 1982 by Houghton Mifflin Co.

The Complete Weather Resource Volume I: Understanding Weather, Phillis Engelbert, Copyright © 1997, The Gale Group

Dakes Annotated Reference Bible, The Old and New Testaments, with notes, concordance and index. Copyright © 1963 by, 1991, Finis Jennings Dake

The Exhaustive Concordance of the Bible, by James Strong, S. T. D., LL. D. Published by Broadman and Holman Publishers, Nashville, TN

Jones' Dictionary of Old Testament Proper Names, Alfred Jones, Copyright © 1997 by Kregel Publications

Number in Scripture: Its Supernatural Design and Spiritual Significance, by E.W. Bullinger, Kregel Publication, Copyright © 1999

Smith's Bible Dictionary Revised Edition, Published by Holman Bible Publishers, Nashville, TN

www.ace.mmu.ac.uk

www.answers.com/topic/agoraphobia

www.archeology.about.com/od/eterms/g/elam.htm

www.bibletools.org//index.cfm/fuseaction/Def.show/RTD/isbe/ID/2927/Elam.htm

www.cais-soas.com/CAIS/History/Elamite/elam_history.htm

www.cais-soas.com/CAIS/Religions/iranian/anahita.htm

www.catholiccity.com/encyclopedia/a/amraphel.html

www.christiananswers.net/dictionary/shinarthelandof.html

www.christnotes.org/dictionary.php?dict=hbn&id=203

www.dragonrest.net/histories/ishtar.html

www.dictionary.law.com

www.dkosopedia.com

www.education.jlab.org

www.en.wikipedia.org/wiki/Elam

www.en.wikipedia.org/wiki/Ishtar

www.en.wikipedia.org/wiki/Shamash

www.en.wikipedia.org/wiki/Shinar

www.en.wikipedia.org/wiki/Susa

www.en.wikipedia-TheFreeEncyclopedia.Elam

www.en.wikipedia.org/wiki/Tidal (Bible King)

www.fundraisingjba.com/givingUSA05findings.htm

www.goliath.ecnext.com/comsite5

www.history-world.org/ancient_civilization.htm

www.history-world.org/larsa.htm

www.holylandnetwork.com/jerusalem/history.htm

www.iranchamber.com//history/elamite/elamite.php

www.jewishencyclopedia.com

www.jewishencyclopedia.com/view.
jsp?artid=1440&letter=A

www.killology.com/article-psychological.htm

www.killology.com/art_weap_sum_avids.htm

www.law.com

www.lexicorient.com

www.library.thinkquest.org

www.mayoclinic.com/health/phobias/DS00272

www.nlm.nih.gov/medlineplus/phobias.html

www.psychology.about.com/od/phobias/a/phobialist.htm

www.pyschologymatters.org/stressimmune.html

www.psywarrior.com/psyhist.html

www.reference.allrefer.com/encyclopedia/L/Larsa.html

www.studylight.org/enc/isb/view.cgi?number=T3017

www.symbols.com/encyclopedia/26/2646.html

www.symbols.com/encyclopedia/28/2824.html

www.syriagate.com/Syria/about/general/history.htm

www.webmd.com/anxiety-panic/specific-phobias

www.wikipedia/mesopotamia.com

www.windows.ucar.
edu/tour/link=/mythology/shamashsun.html&edu=high

www.wondersmith.com/heroes/goddess.htm

www.occultopedia.com/v/venus.htm

www.reference.allrefer.com/encyclopedia/L/Larsa.html

www.rong-chong.com/religions/articles/
elamite_religion.php

www.stargods.org/MA_Giants.html

www.studylight.org/enc/isb/view.cgi?number=T3017

www.symbols.com/encyclopedia/26/2646.html

www.symbols.com/encyclopedia/28/2824.html

www.syriagate.com/Syria/about/general/history.htm

www.truthnet.
org/biblicalarcheology/2/Patriachalpreriod.htm

www.weather.com

www.windows.ucar.
edu/tour/link=/mythology/shamashsun.html&edu=high

www.wondersmith.com/heroes/goddess.htm

www.worldvision.org

www.wsu.edu/`dee/MESO/HITTITES.HTM

978-0-595-46128-8
0-595-46128-X

Printed in the United States
149999LV00004B/19/A